mp
Pa-tient en - dur-ance At-tain-eth to all things;
p
cresc.
mf
Who God pos-sess-eth In
f
mf
noth-ing is want-ing;
mp
p calmo
p
A - lone God suf - fi - ceth.
pp

To Mr. & Mrs. Igor Stravinsky

Let Nothing Disturb Thee

St. Teresa of Avila
English version by
Henry Wadsworth Longfellow

David Diamond